BILLY GRAHAM

Evang~~elisti~~

Dear Friend,

I am pleased to send you ~~...~~ Swindoll, a longtime friend ~~...~~ ~~...~~ ministry. I pray it will give you renewed love for the Savior and hope for the future as you ponder the riches of God's mercy and grace.

This 40-day journey is designed to be used during the season leading up to the celebration of Easter. It's an inspiring reminder of *"the sufferings of Christ and the glories that would follow"* (1 Peter 1:11, NKJV). I believe this biblical account of Jesus' redeeming love will fill you with joy and trust as you walk with Him day by day in the power of His victory over sin and death.

For more than 60 years, the Billy Graham Evangelistic Association has worked to take the Good News of Jesus Christ throughout the world by every effective means available, and I'm excited about what God will do in the years ahead.

We would appreciate knowing how our ministry has touched your life. May God richly bless you.

Sincerely,

Franklin Graham
President

If you would like to know more about our ministry, please contact us:

IN THE U.S.:
Billy Graham Evangelistic Association
1 Billy Graham Parkway
Charlotte, NC 28201-0001
billygraham.org
info@bgea.org
Toll-free: 1-877-247-2426

IN CANADA:
Billy Graham Evangelistic
   Association of Canada
20 Hopewell Way NE
Calgary, AB T3J 5H5
billygraham.ca
Toll-free: 1-888-393-0003

Walk with Jesus

The Journey to the Cross and Beyond

by Charles R. Swindoll

This special edition is published for the
Billy Graham Evangelistic Association
by Thomas Nelson, Inc.

THOMAS NELSON
Since 1798

NASHVILLE   DALLAS   MEXICO CITY   RIO DE JANEIRO

This special edition is published for the Billy Graham Evangelistic Association by Thomas Nelson, Inc.

Published in Nashville, Tennessee, by Thomas Nelson. Thomas Nelson is a registered trademark of Thomas Nelson, Inc.

Published in association with Yates & Yates, www.yates2.com

Portions of this book were adapted from *Jesus: The Greatest Life of ALL* and *The Darkness and the Dawn* by Charles R. Swindoll © 2008. Used by permission.

Unless otherwise noted, Scripture quotations in this book are taken from THE NEW KING JAMES VERSION®. Copyright © 1982 by Thomas Nelson, Inc. Used by permission. All rights reserved.

Scripture references marked KJV are from THE KING JAMES VERSION.

Scripture references marked NET are from the NET BIBLE, NEW ENGLISH TRANSLATION. Copyright 1996–2007 by Biblical Studies Press, LLC. All rights reserved.

Scripture references marked NASB are from the NEW AMERICAN STANDARD BIBLE®, © Copyright The Lockman Foundation1960, 1962, 1963, 1968, 1971, 1972, 1973, 1975, 1977. Used by permission.

Scripture references marked NIV are from the HOLY BIBLE: NEW INTERNATIONAL VERSION®. Copyright © 1973, 1978, 1984 by the International Bible Society. Used by permission of Zondervan Publishing House. All rights reserved.

ISBN: 978-1-4041-7410-8 (BGEA)

Library of Congress Cataloging-in-Publication Data

Swindoll, Charles R.
   Walk with Jesus : a journey to the cross and beyond / Charles R. Swindoll.
      p. cm.
   ISBN: 978-1-4002-0247-8
   1. Jesus Christ--Passion—Meditations. 2. Jesus Christ—Meditations.
I. Title.
BT431.3.S96   2008
232.96—dc22   2008045174

Printed in the United States of America
11 12 13 14 BTY 6 5 4 3 2 1

Contents

~~~~

Introduction

~∂∞~

All historians accept the fact that Jesus existed and that He was a Galilean Jew who lived and taught during the first century. Many would also agree that He was martyred because His teachings were so radical and controversial. Most, however, would not agree on what He taught, because, from their point of view, successive generations of His followers reshaped, amplified, and systematized His teaching into what we know today as Christianity.

Hopefully, as you walk with Jesus during these next forty days, His life and sacrifice for your sake and mine will bring to light a deeper relationship and purpose in your life with Jesus Christ.

Let us begin with the Pharisees' plot to kill Jesus and rid themselves of this man who claimed to be the Son of God.

Day 1 - The Plot to Kill Jesus

~∂∞~

For many months, storm clouds had been gathering over Jerusalem. Jesus focused His attention on Galilee during the early part of His ministry, but He regularly traveled to the Holy City in Judea to celebrate the more than half-dozen Jewish feasts throughout the year. And each visit intensified the grow-

ing tension between Jesus and the religious establishment—
the Sadducees, with their control of the temple, and the Pharisees, who had a grip on the people.

The disciples could sense the danger mounting. So when
Jesus announced that they would travel to visit Martha and
Mary in the village of Bethany, just two miles from Jersusalem,
Thomas turned to the other disciples and shrugged. "Let us
also go, that we may die with him" (John 11:16). The disciples'
fear was not unfounded. On their last visit, an angry mob
sought to stone their Master.

After Jesus raised Lazarus from the dead, He won a new as-
sembly of followers. However, several friends of the Pharisees
saw His growing popularity as a threat and scurried to
Jerusalem with the news.

> So the chief priests [Sadducees] and the Pharisees called
> the council together and said, "What are we doing? For
> this man is performing many miraculous signs. If we
> allow him to go on in this way, everyone will believe in
> him, and the Romans will come and take away our sanc-
> tuary and our nation."
>
> Then one of them, Caiaphas, who was high priest that
> year, said, "You know nothing at all! You do not realize
> that it is more to your advantage to have one man die for
> the people than for the whole nation to perish."
>
> —John 11:47–50 NET

With that, the plot to kill Jesus began.

The religious leaders would have to be crafty. They didn't
dare seize Him in public for fear that the ever-growing multitude of His followers would turn on them and revolt. And

nothing would bring down the wrath of Rome quicker than insurrection.

$\mathcal{D}ay\ 2$ - Hail, King Jesus!

Imagine the seething consternation of the religious authorities when Jesus arrived in Jerusalem to celebrate the Passover feast. He deliberately chose to ride a humble foal of a donkey, not only a recognized symbol of peace, but a glaring reference to the messianic prophecy of Zechariah.

> *"Rejoice greatly, O daughter of Zion!*
> *Shout, O daughter of Jerusalem!*
> *Behold, your King is coming to you;*
> *He is just and having salvation,*
> *Lowly and riding on a donkey,*
> *A colt, the foal of a donkey.*
> *I will cut off the chariot from Ephraim*
> *And the horse from Jerusalem;*
> *The battle bow shall be cut off.*
> *He shall speak peace to the nations;*
> *His dominion shall be 'from sea to sea,*
> *And from the River to the ends of the earth.'"*
> —Zechariah 9:9–10 (NKJV)

The religious rulers clearly understood the message this sent. It said, in effect, *I'm coming in peace as your Messiah, Israel's priest-king. Yield your authority to Me, and let's begin building the new kingdom.* Thousands of Jesus' followers responded to the gesture by giving Him a welcome reserved for royalty. They lined the road leading into the city, cheered His name, and paved His path with their cloaks and cut palm branches. They shouted, *"Hosanna!"* which means, *"Save us now!"*

Day 3 - The Historical Anticipation of the Coming Messiah

∽∾∽

The stone which the builders rejected
Has become the chief cornerstone.
This was the LORD's doing;
It is marvelous in our eyes.
This is the day the LORD has made;
We will rejoice and be glad in it.
Save now, I pray, O LORD;
O Lord, I pray, send now prosperity.
Blessed is he who comes in the name of the LORD!
We have blessed you from the house of the LORD.
God is the LORD,
And He has given us light;
Bind the sacrifice with cords to the horns of the altar.

—Psalm 118:22–27 (NKJV)

On previous occasions, Jesus worshiped in the temple and taught willing hearers. When challenged by the religious elite, He responded, but never at the expense of His mission of teaching and preaching. He taught against the corruption He saw there and even disrupted their business more than once. But this time was different. This time He came to claim authority over the temple and to take His stand against the organized crime of Annas, the power broker behind the office of high priest.

At one point during the tumultuous week after His arrival, Jesus sat to teach in the temple. As a large group of followers and conspirators gathered around the daring rabbi to hear a parable, He captured their attention with His opening words: *"There was a certain landowner who planted a vineyard and set a hedge around it, dug a winepress in it and built a tower"* (Matthew 21:33 NKJV).

Most of the images in Jesus' teaching drew upon the common experience of Jews living in the first century: shepherd and sheep, sewer and seed, wine and wineskins, master and servants. But no metaphor touched the Hebrew soul like the picture of the vinedresser and his vineyard.

Day 4 - The True Vine

I am the true vine, and My Father is the vinedresser. Every branch in Me that does not bear fruit He takes away; and every branch that bears fruit He prunes, that it may bear more fruit.

—John 15:1–2

Each year, the Hebrew people celebrated Passover with a week-long festival—the combined observance of the Passover Feast and the Feast of Unleavened Bread. For nearly two thousand years, they paused annually to commemorate their ancestors' liberation from Egypt and God's planting them in the Promised Land. Jesus gathered His disciples in a specially prepared room for what He knew to be His last time with them before His death. At this final meal celebrating God's faithfulness to Israel, He would summarize His teaching, prepare His disciples to carry on His ministry, and give the familiar rituals of the Passover celebration a new significance.

After reiterating His earlier prediction that He would be beaten and murdered by the religious leaders in Jerusalem, Jesus returned to an earlier theme to illustrate how His relationship with the disciples would continue nonetheless. *"I am the true vine, and My Father is the vinedresser"* (John 15:1).

Compare this vineyard parable to the others and you will see a dramatic recasting of the images. In this version, Jesus took the place of Israel, claiming to be the authentic, healthy vine the nation had failed to become. The kingdom of God was its king.

Day 5 - Being in Christ

You are already clean because of the word that I have spoken to you. Abide in Me, and I in you. As the branch cannot bear fruit of itself, unless it abides in the vine, neither can you, unless you abide in Me.

—John 15:3–4

Being "in Christ" puts the person in right relationship with the Father. Paul says, *"There is now no condemnation to them which are in Christ Jesus"* (Romans 8:1 KJV). The believer is regarded as having the same righteous standing as Jesus. With the believer's eternal destiny secure, Jesus turned from the issue of position—"in Me"—to that of production. The purpose of a branch is no different than that of the vine: to produce fruit. Jesus said, *"Every branch in Me that does not bear fruit He takes away"* (John 15:2).

Many versions of the Bible translate a key Greek term in this verse as "takes away," "removes," or even "cuts off," but its primary definition is "to lift from the ground."[1] The word can and often does mean "to lift with a view to carrying, to carry off or put away."[2] In keeping with the metaphor, Jesus most likely referred to the vinedresser's practice of lifting a sagging branch and tying it to the trellis—a procedure called "training." The vinedresser also carefully prunes the branches to encourage healthy growth.

Interpreting a parable demands we appreciate the richness of the story's imagery without seeing more than the author intended. Stare at anything long enough, and it will bear the imprint of your imagination. So we must restrain ourselves from seeing more than what the parable says. Jesus did not identify what the fruit represents. Some have suggested that the fruit of a believer is another believer—in other words, a person has chosen to place his or her faith in Jesus Christ as a result of a believer's influence. This may be what Jesus had in mind, but "fruit" may also refer to another noteworthy product.

Day 6 - The New Vineyard

❧

If you abide in Me, and My words abide in you, you will ask what you desire, and it shall be done for you. By this

My Father is glorified, that you bear much fruit; so you will be My disciples.

—John 15:7–8

Jesus came to do what neither Israel nor we can do. Now, He is the vineyard, and He will be faithful to bear fruit. And He invites us to attach ourselves to Him, like a branch abiding in a vine, so that we can become a part of this great fruit-bearing enterprise. This is not referring to salvation. By the time of His last evening with His disciples, the issue of salvation had been settled. This is a matter of living abundantly and producing a bumper crop of Christlike qualities in our character.

If your eternal destiny has been sealed by your belief in Christ, the crucial question for you is how you will live now? Will you try to become good and righteous on your own … and become good for nothing? Or will you abide in Christ … and allow Him to produce good within you?

That evening as Jesus broke unleavened bread and called it His body, and as He poured the ceremonial wine and called it His blood, He invited His disciples to eat and drink. He used this—yet another symbol—to teach His followers that life must come from Him.

Day 7 - The Gathering Storm

Jesus never regarded His path to the cross as anything but the successful unfolding of a plan. He had said early in His ministry, *"Do not think that I came to bring peace on earth. I did not come to bring peace but a sword"* (Matthew 10:34). The sword of which

He spoke is the sharpest of all implements of conflict: truth. And those who hold it will find themselves hunted by evil.

After feeding the five thousand men and their families in the hill country of Galilee, Jesus rendezvoused with His disciples on the waves of the nearby sea and then sailed to Capernaum. Meanwhile, the multitudes frantically tried to trace His steps and finally deduced that He must have accompanied the disciples back to the hometown of Peter, Andrew, James, and John.

They arrived to find Jesus teaching in the synagogue. They then confronted Him with the suspicion that He had deliberately eluded them, but Jesus returned their objections with an indictment.

> *"Most assuredly, I say to you, you seek Me, not because you saw the signs, but because you ate of the loaves and were filled. Do not labor for the food which perishes, but for the food which endures to everlasting life, which the Son of Man will give you, because God the Father has set His seal on Him."*
>
> —John 6:26–27

To the Jews gathered around Jesus in the synagogue, the rebuke echoed the voice of Moses, who had challenged the wandering generation of Israelites.

$\mathcal{D}ay$ 8 - The Battle Line Between Good and Evil

❧

Then Jesus said to them, "Most assuredly, I say to you, Moses did not give you the bread from heaven, but My

> *Father gives you the true bread from heaven. For the bread of God is He who comes down from heaven and gives life to the world." And Jesus said to them, "I am the bread of life. He who comes to Me shall never hunger, and he who believes in Me shall never thirst."*
>
> —John 6:32–33, 35

The battle line between good and evil doesn't run along borders or around races or even across thresholds. The cosmic battle between good and evil divides heart from heart without discrimination, for each person chooses his or her side. Oddly, it is not a choice between truth and untruth—God would never require a darkened mind to make such a choice. That would be crueler than requiring a paralytic to drag himself to a pool in a race for healing. We choose by how we respond to the Redeemer, who holds out something we innately know to be missing within. Those who push it away do so knowingly. At some point in every life, ignorance ceases to be the issue, and we either choose to heed the voice resonating in the hollows of our soul or we opt for willful disobedience.

That's why Jesus said, *"Do not think that I came to bring peace on earth. I did not come to bring peace but a sword. For I have come to 'set a man against his father, a daughter against her mother, and a daughter-in-law against her mother-in-law'; and 'a man's enemies will be those of his own household'"* (Matthew 10:34–36). Obviously God wants families together, but, unfortunately, the truth of Jesus Christ is a divider. On most issues, there are many shades of gray, but not this one. And the whole world—right down to the individual households—has been partitioned into realms, that of light and darkness.

What must we do to accomplish the deeds God requires?

Jesus said, *"This is the work of God, that you believe in Him whom He sent"* (John 6:29). With the arrival of Jesus Christ, the kingdom of God ceased to be one defined by geography, but one established in the hearts of those who choose to believe.

$\mathcal{D}ay$ *9* - The Blind Guides

The division between Jesus and the Pharisees had never been anything less than a canyon. He came to speak truth; they desired control. And one thing will always be true of controllers: what they cannot control, they destroy.

While Jesus was still ministering in Galilee, an envoy of Pharisees traveled from Jerusalem to meet with Jesus on a matter of grave concern to them. They likely felt it was a mission of mercy in which they would redeem a wayward rabbi. Of course, people who seek control don't see the world in terms of conformity with truth or untruth, but in terms of agreement with them.

> *Why do Your disciples transgress the tradition of the elders? For they do not wash their hands when they eat bread.*
>
> —Matthew 15:2

This body of strict traditions eventually supplanted the very Law it was intended to uphold. And by the time of Jesus, failure to observe this tradition was regarded as disobedience to the law of God. Furthermore, this man-made religiosity became the means by which the Pharisees maintained the illusion of moral superiority. Ironically, their religious zeal put them at odds with God. Not only were they motivated by lust for power, but their traditions very often violated the very Law they supposedly cherished.

> *[Jesus] answered them, "And why do you disobey the commandment of God because of your tradition? For God said, 'Honor your father and mother' and 'Whoever insults his father or mother must be put to death.' But you say, 'If someone tells his father or mother, "Whatever help you would have received from me is given to God,"' he does not need to honor his father.' You have nullified the word of God on account of tradition. Hypocrites!*
> *Isaiah prophesied correctly about you when he said,*
> *'This people honors me with their lips,*
> *but their heart is far from me,*
> *and they worship me in vain,*
> *teaching as doctrines the commandments of men.'"*
> —Matthew 15:3–9 NET

The sword of truth has but one target: the heart. And when the heart of a hypocrite is pierced, it bleeds resentment ... ultimately, hatred. Jesus concluded His rebuke with a clarification. *"Hear and understand: Not what goes into the mouth defiles a man; but what comes out of the mouth, this defiles a man"* (Matthew 15:10–11).

Day 10 - "Woe to You"

The triumphal entry of Jesus to the capital of the Hebrews marked a change in His relationship to the Holy City. He no longer visited as a worshiper; He claimed it as King. His subjects had strewn His path to the city with cut palm branches and their own cloaks, shouting "Hosanna!" which means "Save us!"

While the people cheered, Jesus wept.

> *"If you had known, even you, especially in this your day,*
> *the things that make for your peace! But now they are*
> *hidden from your eyes. For days will come upon you*
> *when your enemies will build an embankment around*
> *you, surround you and close you in on every side, and*
> *level you, and your children within you, to the ground;*
> *and they will not leave in you one stone upon another,*
> *because you did not know the time of your visitation."*
> —Luke 19:42–44

Jesus' first official act came shortly after arriving in the temple. On several occasions, He had spoken against the corruption taking place in the outer courts, an institution known as the Annas Bazaar, but that was before assuming office.

Annas retreated from public view but continued to control every Jewish political office in Jerusalem, including that of high priest. After his removal from office, no fewer than five sons and a grandson succeeded him, and at the time of Jesus, his son-in-law, Caiaphas, ran the temple.

Day 11 - The Temple

Then Jesus went into the temple of God and drove
out all those who bought and sold in the temple, and

> *overturned the tables of the money changers and the*
> *seats of those who sold doves. And He said to them, "It is*
> *written, 'My house shall be called a house of prayer,' but*
> *you have made it a 'den of thieves.'"*

—Matthew 21:12–13

The Sadducees—the skirmishing collection of rivals and pawns of Annas—found in Jesus a common enemy. None of them appreciated His shutting down their money machine. Consequently, *"the chief priests, the scribes, and the leaders of the people sought to destroy Him, and were unable to do anything; for all the people were very attentive to hear Him"* (Luke 19:47–48).

After cleansing the temple courts of the Sadducees' corruption, Jesus called the Pharisees' hypocrisy into account.

The Pharisees anticipated the arrival of a conquering Messiah. Their tradition said He would come suddenly to His temple. Indeed, He had arrived, but not as they had expected. Jesus forcefully handed down what could very well be the sharpest rebuke recorded in Scripture. Eight times He uttered "woe," an exclamation used to express deep, anguished sorrow over something grievous. Seven times He called them "scribes and Pharisees, hypocrites." Five times He called them "blind." And in this stinging indictment, Jesus spelled out a detailed catalog of sins that had been plainly evident for years but gone unchecked for fear of retribution. But no more. The true Messiah had come to take His stand for truth in the place where truth was being trampled.

Day 12 - Four Lessons for Truth Tellers

∽◦∾

Few weapons against evil can rival the sword of truth. Though readily available to anyone brave enough to hold it, few will. And it's little wonder. The privilege of wielding so powerful a tool comes at great cost—misunderstandings, false accusations, broken relationships, loneliness, frustration. Furthermore, standing for what's right frequently involves terrifying bouts with self-doubt and even self-recrimination. Sometimes the choice to take truth by the handle results in glorious victory, but more often the counterstrike of evil comes with startling ferocity and lasting devastation.

First, *knowing your mission will help you stay focused on the goal.* Jesus clearly understood the reason for His coming to earth and never allowed popularity, success, opposition, threats, or even dissention within His ranks to distract Him. He remained steadfastly focused on that mission, though not without due care for those around Him. He worked hard to make the truth plain. He often repeated the invitation to embrace the truth. But He never allowed the failure of others to pull Him off course.

Second, *encountering evil requires confrontation.* Few people enjoy confrontation, but standing for the truth against evil will inevitably require it. And sometimes what must be said will be difficult to say as well as difficult for others to hear. Only rarely—perhaps once in a lifetime—will confrontation require the kind of severe rebuke Jesus brought against the Pharisees. The greater the evil, the stronger must be the confrontation. In general, I advise kindness unless a kind approach is irrespon-sible, but never kindness at the expense of plain talk.

Be prepared to state the truth plainly.

Third, *boldness in the course of a noble fight is worth the risk.* Standing for truth requires boldness. Some will be offended by it, so expect to be criticized for style when the opposition can find no fault with content. Furthermore, boldness may require strong action to accompany strong speech. You may have to quit a job, end a relationship, confront a powerful opponent, cope with a fear, deal with threats, perhaps even face certain defeat. Don't back down. If you stand on truth, you'll only regret your timidity later, but you'll never regret being bold.

Fourth, *truth telling offers no guarantee of victory.* We live in a world that does not operate according to God's rules. The present world system punishes good deeds and rewards those who choose evil. In the words of James Russell Lowell, "Truth forever on the scaffold; wrong forever on the throne."[3]

A two-fisted grip on the sword of truth, while sacrificial, does offer great reward. Truth grants freedom from guilt and shame. Truth breeds contentment, instills confidence, stimulates creativity, fosters intimacy, encourages honesty, inspires courage, and sets people free. But, most importantly, it puts us on God's side of the issue. We have His promise that He will amply reward any sac-rifice that truth demands, if not in this life, then certainly the next.

Day 13 - The Last Supper

Thursday evening, just before sundown, the Master and His disciples arrived in their festive, white tunics. As they entered the room, a servant should have been available to help them loosen their sandals and rinse their feet. But they were alone. The disciples chattered and laughed as each lay down on a cushion and propped himself on one elbow near the table. Only two of them knew this would be their last meal together: Jesus and His betrayer.

After Jesus settled into the honored place reserved for Him at the head of the table, He lit the ceremonial lamp to signify the end of work and beginning of celebration. He filled a cup of wine, the first of four ceremonial cups for the evening, and held it up. He gave thanks to the Father for His faithfulness to Israel and then dedicated the evening to remembering the Exodus. As each man drained his cup and then reached for a bowl of water for the first ceremonial washing of hands, Jesus stood up, removed His outer tunic, and wrapped a towel around His waist. After retrieving the pitcher and basin from the servant's station, He assumed a servant's position at one disciple's feet, rinsed them clean, dried them with the towel, and then silently moved to the next. As He knelt before Peter, the brash disciple pulled away and said, *"Never shall You wash my feet!"*

Jesus said to him, "He who is bathed needs only to wash his feet, but is completely clean; and you are clean, but not all of you." For He knew who would betray Him; therefore He said, "You are not all clean."

So when He had washed their feet, taken His garments, and sat down again, He said to them, "Do you know what I have done to you? You call Me Teacher and Lord, and you say well, for so I am. If I then, your Lord and Teacher, have washed your feet, you also ought to wash one another's feet. For I have given you an

*example, that you should do as I have done to you. Most
assuredly, I say to you, a servant is not greater than his
master; nor is he who is sent greater than he who sent
him. If you know these things, blessed are you if you do
them.*

"*I do not speak concerning all of you. I know whom I
have chosen; but that the Scripture may be fulfilled, 'He
who eats bread with Me has lifted up his heel against Me.'*"

—John 13:10–18

Day 14 - In the Garden

They left the Upper Room and made their way to a familiar re-
treat, a private garden called Gethsemane on the Mount of Olives,
just across the Kidron Valley from Jerusalem. Soon after passing
through the entrance of the little garden, Jesus asked His disciples to pray for Him while He sought comfort from His Father. He
asked Peter, James, and John to follow Him a little farther, then
said, "*My soul is exceedingly sorrowful, even to death. Stay here and
watch with Me*" (Matthew 26:38). Then He disappeared into the
darkness.

Jesus wrestled with temptation. The terror of His coming
ordeal gripped Him mercilessly. His blood dripped like sweat
through the pores of His skin. As He stumbled through the
darkness at Gethsemane, occasionally staggering and falling,
thoughts kept returning to challenge His resolve. Why should
He have to suffer on behalf of humanity? No moral imperative
required God to sacrifice His Son. He would be no less holy or
righteous if He allowed the race of sin-sick humans to suffer

the just consequences of their own rebellion. Nothing compelled Jesus to complete the mission—nothing, that is, except love for the people He had made and obedience to His Father.

> *Then Jesus came with them to a place called Gethsemane, and said to the disciples, "Sit here while I go and pray over there." And He took with Him Peter and the two sons of Zebedee, and He began to be sorrowful and deeply distressed. Then He said to them, "My soul is exceedingly sorrowful, even to death. Stay here and watch with Me."*
> *He went a little farther and fell on His face, and prayed, saying, "O My Father, if it is possible, let this cup pass from Me; nevertheless, not as I will, but as You will."*
> —Matthew 26:36–39

But no sooner would Jesus submit to the plan of the Father than the temptation would seize Him again. No fewer than three distinct times would He have to submit. Each temptation was met with the same resolve: *"Not as I will, but as You will."*

Day 15 - The Betrayal

> *Then He came to His disciples and said to them, "Are you still sleeping and resting? Behold, the hour is at hand, and the Son of Man is being betrayed into the hands of sinners. Rise, let us be going. See, My betrayer is at hand."*
> *And while He was still speaking, behold, Judas, one of the twelve, with a great multitude with swords and clubs,*

came from the chief priests and elders of the people. Now
His betrayer had given them a sign, saying, "Whomever I
kiss, He is the One; seize Him." Immediately he went up
to Jesus and said, "Greetings, Rabbi!" and kissed Him.
                                                —Matthew 26:45–49

Just then, Judas emerged out of the shadows alone. "Greetings, Rabbi!" He bowed to his Master and began smothering Jesus' hands and cheeks with nervous, enthusiastic kisses. Incredulous, Jesus responded, *"Judas, are you betraying the Son of Man with a kiss?"* (Luke 22:48). *"Friend, why have you come?"* (Matthew 26:50). But Judas stood silent and motionless. He had done his part. Finally, Jesus moved away and called into the darkness, "Whom do you seek?"

"Jesus the Nazarene," a voice shouted back.

"I am He."

The glimmer of torches emerged from the darkness and cautiously weaved their way through the trees as the disciples instinctively formed a circle around Jesus. Peter quietly drew a short sword from its sheath and hid it in the folds of his tunic. Eventually, the light of a hundred or more flames flooded the clearing and glinted off a forest of swords and spears.

Jesus searched the faces in the crowd for a commanding officer. "Whom do you seek?"

The captain of the temple guard stepped forward. "Jesus the Nazarene."

"I told you that I am He; so if you seek Me, let these go their way."

$\mathscr{D}ay$ *16* - The Surrender

The captain motioned and three men moved toward Jesus with a set of chains. Suddenly, Peter flung his sword high above his head, lunged toward the lead soldier, and brought it down hard, aiming for the center of his head. The blade glanced off the side of his helmet and lopped off his exposed right ear. Peter drew back for another lunge when Jesus shouted, *"Stop! No more of this"* (Luke 22:51 NASB). Jesus commanded Peter, *"Put your sword in the sheath. Shall I not drink the cup the Father has given me?"* (John 18:11).

Jesus tenderly reached for the injured soldier, who stood clutching the side of his head, and gently pulled his hand away. As He repositioned the dangling mass of flesh, He said to no one in particular, *"Have you come out, as against a robber, with swords and clubs? When I was with you daily in the temple, you did not try to seize Me. But this is your hour, and the power of darkness"* (Luke 22:52–53).

Once the man's ear had been restored, Jesus held out His arms and allowed a soldier to place irons on His wrists and ankles. By the time the soldiers led Jesus down the side of the mountain toward Jerusalem, most of the disciples had scattered and fled into the night. No one was quite sure what had happened to Judas.

$\mathscr{D}ay$ *17* - Before the Trial of Jesus

Jesus was too popular to assassinate. One word from the disciples might have ignited the powder keg of popular resentment that lay beneath Jerusalem. And the leaders dared not turn Him into a martyr for fear of making Him even more influential in death than in life. So they hatched a plan to discredit Him as a blaspheming kook and have Him publicly executed in the most shameful manner possible.

They needed to do everything out of the public eye, but that proved difficult. Jesus stopped traveling in public except when protected by the adoration of the multitudes. And no one except His closest companions knew where He would be most vulnerable to attack. So, when Judas approached them with his scheme, they quickly struck a bargain. They signed on to a nighttime arrest of Jesus in exchange for thirty silver coins— roughly four months' wages for an unskilled worker or the redemption price of a common slave.

From the first moment of His arrest, Jesus conducted Himself with utmost dignity yet never backed away from speaking the truth with gentle candor. *"Have you come out, as against a robber, with swords and clubs? When I was with you daily in the temple, you did not try to seize Me. But this is your hour, and the power of darkness"* (Luke 22:52–53). Of course, they all knew what they had chosen to do was wrong or they would have done it by day and in full view of the multitudes. Nevertheless, Jesus understood His mission and that truth has its consequences. He never wavered. Looking at Peter, He said, *"Shall I not drink the cup which My Father has given Me?"* (John 18:11).

Day 18 - The First Trial of Jesus
∽◦∾

Once the commander of the temple guard had Jesus bound, he

and the small army led Him down the Mount of Olives, across the Kidron Valley, into Jerusalem, and straight to the home of Annas. Though the old patriarch no longer ruled as high priest, he remained the head of a vast empire of organized corruption in Jerusalem. "He and his family were proverbial for their rapacity and greed."[4]

When Jesus cleansed the temple of what he called "robbers," several religious authorities demanded to know, *"By what authority are You doing these things? And who gave You this authority?"* (Matthew 21:23). Understandably, they could not imagine one man challenging the Annas crime family. This was why Jesus wasn't taken to jail or to the Jewish council or to the duly appointed high priest or even to the Roman procurator. He stood alone before the godfather of Jerusalem.

The soldiers positioned Jesus before an empty chair in the great hall of Annas's house and then stood a few paces away on either side. After a short pause, Annas entered, fully dressed, even though it was a little after midnight. He took his seat and arranged his robes before raising his eyes to find Jesus looking straight at them.

> *The high priest then asked Jesus about His disciples and His doctrine. Jesus answered him, "I spoke openly to the world. I always taught in synagogues and in the temple, where the Jews always meet, and in secret I have said nothing. Why do you ask Me? Ask those who have heard Me what I said to them. Indeed they know what I said."*
> —John 18:19–21

Day 19 - The Response of Jesus

❦

At first glance, Jesus appears to offer a curt response. In reality, He merely objected to no fewer than a half-dozen points of order in the proceedings. The trial took place at night, during the week of Passover, behind closed doors, and away from the temple. If Annas were going to pretend he had jurisdiction and presume to play the role of high priest, he was not to participate in questioning, and the answers he sought would have compelled the accused to testify against himself. Furthermore, as Jesus pointed out, witnesses should have been easy to find, but none had been summoned.

> *And when He had said these things, one of the officers who stood by struck Jesus with the palm of his hand, saying, "Do You answer the high priest like that?" Jesus answered him, "If I have spoken evil, bear witness of the evil; but if well, why do you strike Me?"*
>
> —John 18:22–23

Jesus again pointed to the fact that no one had testified against Him and that He wasn't guilty of anything more than allowing Annas to make a fool of himself. Clearly, the object of the trial was not to discover truth or render a just verdict; therefore Jesus refused to cooperate with the mockery they were making of Jewish law. Without another word, *"Annas sent Him bound to Caiaphas the high priest"* (John 18:24).

$\mathscr{D}\!ay$ 20 - The Second Trial of Jesus

Because Jesus presented such a serious challenge to the authority of the Sanhedrin, Caiaphas had little trouble convening the council in the wee hours of the morning. While Annas questioned Jesus, most if not all of the seventy members filled a large upper chamber in the high priest's palace. They presumably met for the purpose of hearing a case against Jesus, but His destiny had been decided long before He arrived.

The Sanhedrin pressed their case against Jesus, which was itself a violation of the council's own rules. According to their law, the role of the Sanhedrin was to presume innocence and even argue for the acquittal until accusers and corroborating witnesses left them no alternative than to convict the defendant. Witnesses were to be questioned individually, and if their stories conflicted, both testimonies were to be thrown out. The high priest was to preside over the trial, facilitate debate among the seventy members, and was forbidden to question the accused. And no defendant was ever required to testify against himself. Nevertheless ...

Now the chief priests and all the council sought testimony against Jesus to put Him to death, but found none. For many bore false witness against Him, but their testimonies did not agree. Then some rose up and bore false witness against Him, saying, "We heard Him say, 'I will destroy this temple made with hands, and within three days I will build another made without hands.'" But not even then did their testimony agree. And the high priest stood up in the midst and asked Jesus, saying, "Do You answer nothing? What is it these men testify against You?" But He kept silent and answered nothing.

Again the high priest asked Him, saying to Him, "Are You the Christ, the Son of the Blessed?" Jesus said, "I am. And you will see the Son of Man sitting at the right hand of the Power, and coming with the clouds of heaven." Then the high priest tore his clothes and said, "What further need do we have of witnesses? You have heard the blasphemy! What do you think?"

And they all condemned Him to be deserving of death.

—Mark 14:55–64

Day 21 - Peter's Denial

As the soldiers and a larger collection of servants sought refuge from the chilly night air around a fire, Peter avoided making eye contact and spoke as little as possible. However, one of the servants had apparently spoken to the gatekeeper at the home of Annas and had whispered the news to the others. Eventually, someone put the question to him directly.

Now as Peter was below in the courtyard, one of the servant girls of the high priest came. And when she saw Peter warming himself, she looked at him and said, "You also were with Jesus of Nazareth." But he denied it, saying, "I neither know nor understand what you are saying." And he went out on the porch, and a rooster crowed.

—Mark 14:66–68

The doors to Caiaphas's palace flung open, and the murmuring dignitaries spilled out into the courtyard. John emerged in time to find Peter embroiled in a debate with the crowd of servants and soldiers.

> *"Surely this fellow also was with Him, for he is a Galilean."* Peter insisted, *"Man, I do not know what you are saying!"*
> (Luke 22:59–60)
> *"Surely you also are one of them, for your speech betrays you."* Peter began to swear oaths and call down divine curses upon himself if he were lying. *"I do not know the Man!"*
>
> (Matthew 26:73–74)

Just then, the second call of a rooster drew Peter's attention to the east. The blue-grey seam that separates the black of night from the glow of dawn was just beginning to show along the horizon. And with the light of day came the realization that Peter had not only abandoned his Lord but had sought the camaraderie of those who desired to see Him dead. As the guards pushed Jesus outside, the commotion at the door drew Peter's attention, and his eyes immediately locked onto those of his Master. Then a memory washed over him and rinsed him clean of any pride or confidence in his own faithfulness. The verbal flashback drove a sharp stake of shame into his heart:

> *"Simon, Simon! Indeed, Satan has asked for you, that he may sift you as wheat. But I have prayed for you, that your faith should not fail; and when you have returned to Me, strengthen your brethren." But he said to Him, "Lord, I am ready to go with You, both to prison and to death."*

*Then He said, "I tell you, Peter, the rooster shall not crow
this day before you will deny three times that you know
Me."*

—Luke 22:31–34

Feeling the utter humiliation of his boast, *"Even if all are
made to stumble, yet I will not be,"* (Mark 14:29), Peter fled the
courtyard and wept bitterly for days.

$\mathcal{D}ay$ 22 - The Third Trial of Jesus

By the time the Sanhedrin had adjourned for the night, the sun
was rising on the next day, and they had found their charge:
treason against Rome. They feared Jesus' popularity, suppos-
ing that a word from Him would spark rebellion and bring the
wrath of Rome down on all of them. More than three years
prior to the trials, Caiaphas had inadvertently spoken a
prophecy that he, himself, would fulfill.

*Then the chief priests and the Pharisees gathered a coun-
cil and said, "What shall we do? For this Man works
many signs. If we let Him alone like this, everyone will
believe in Him, and the Romans will come and take
away both our place and nation."*

*And one of them, Caiaphas, being high priest that year,
said to them, "You know nothing at all, nor do you consider that it is expedient for us that one man should die for
the people, and not that the whole nation should perish."*

—John 11:47–50

With the specific charge determined and the verdict already decided, the high priest summoned the council to the official place of judgment, a semicircular hall at the east end of the Royal Portico of the temple. The place was designed to resemble a threshing floor. In ancient times, the place where farmers separated wheat from chaff became the forum where all matters of justice were aired before the entire community.

Day 23 - Jesus Is the Messiah

Finally in the light of day, and finally in the proper venue, and finally before the eyes of the public, the third trial began. Still, the religious leaders violated their own rules. The arbiters of justice were also the accusers. No one advocated for the accused. The trial took place during the Feast of Unleavened Bread, part of the Passover festival. And they compelled the accused to testify against Himself. The purpose of the trial was merely show. The council quickly played out before the public what they had already rehearsed in private.

As soon as it was day, the elders of the people, both chief priests and scribes, came together and led Him into their council, saying, "If You are the Christ, tell us."

But He said to them, "If I tell you, you will by no means believe. And if I also ask you, you will by no means answer Me or let Me go. Hereafter the Son of Man will sit on the right hand of the power of God."

Then they all said, "Are You then the Son of God?"

So He said to them, "You rightly say that I am."
—Luke 22:66–70

Each time Jesus parted His lips to answer, He called attention to the impropriety of the proceedings without denying His claim to be the Messiah. He agreed to their assessment that He claimed the right of kingship, but He would not accept the implications they attached to the charge. Insurrection had never been a part of His plan.

Because truth had never been their object, the council closed the case against Jesus.

> *And they said, "What further testimony do we need? For we have heard it ourselves from His own mouth."*
>
> —Luke 22:71

Day 24 - Encouragement Through Suffering

∽∾

Very few situations in life are more frustrating than suffering injustice alone and unnoticed. Feelings of outrage demand justice. Bitterness demands revenge. Hopelessness begs heaven for relief. Loneliness screams to be heard as a watching world stands aloof. During those dark, painful, lonely times, the silence from heaven can be deafening.

If this is presently your experience, rest assured, you are not alone. The Lord does see your suffering, and He will not allow it to go unanswered. He will see justice done, though perhaps not at the time or in the manner you would prefer. Nevertheless, the agony you suffer, though it feels overwhelming, will not go to waste. If you allow it, this experience can be the means by which God brings you His greatest blessings.

The apostle Peter stood at a distance watching his Master endure the greatest injustice ever suffered. No one was ever more innocent than Jesus. Few were ever more hypocritical and corrupt than Annas and Caiaphas. Perhaps reflecting on how Jesus conducted Himself during that awful time, Peter later wrote to persecuted Christians, *"For what credit is it if, when you are beaten for your faults, you take it patiently? But when you do good and suffer, if you take it patiently, this is commendable before God"* (1 Peter 2:20).

What are the messages in that to us twenty centuries later? Stop trying to be heard. Stop hoping for vindication. Speak the truth, in love and without apology, to whoever will listen. Expect to suffer for doing so. Then quietly and calmly submit yourself to the sovereign will of God.

Jesus accepted that He would not receive justice from men. He knew that the world was then—as it is now—dominated by sin and governed by fallen people. So He did not look to the courts for justice or to the approval of people for affirmation. He instead submitted Himself to the will of the Father. He spoke the truth and refused to allow anger or bitterness to distract anyone from seeing it—should anyone truly desire to see. Throughout the ordeal, He entrusted Himself to the One who will ultimately and inevitably judge every soul righteously. What a magnificent model to follow!

$\mathscr{D}ay$ 25 - The Fourth Trial of Jesus

With the Jewish Passover celebration in full swing and Jerusalem packed with nearly ten times its normal population, Pilate took up residence in the Praetorium to ensure law and order. Nevertheless, he was surprised to hear the Jews clamoring for an audience during the feast. Their concern for ritual purity wouldn't allow them to enter the Roman building, so he had to meet them in the courtyard, which had nearly filled to capacity. Seventy-plus Jewish elders, dressed in their finest regalia, stood in a semicircle around a chained prisoner. The swelling and dried blood on the man's face and the angry crowd behind the elders let the procurator know he should take the early morning audience seriously.

> *Pilate then went out to them and said, "What accusation do you bring against this Man?" They answered and said to him, "If He were not an evildoer, we would not have delivered Him up to you." Then Pilate said to them, "You take Him and judge Him according to your law."*
>
> *Therefore the Jews said to him, "It is not lawful for us to put anyone to death."*

—John 18:29–31

The Jewish leaders recognized that Rome cared only about Rome, so they would have to present Pilate with charges that portrayed Jesus a threat to the state.

And they began to accuse Him, saying, "We found this fellow perverting the nation, and forbidding to pay taxes to Caesar, saying that He Himself is Christ, a King."

—Luke 23:2

Then Pilate entered the Praetorium again, called Jesus, and said to Him, "Are You the King of the Jews?" Jesus answered him, "Are you speaking for yourself about this, or did others tell you this concerning Me?" Pilate answered, "Am I a Jew? Your own nation and the chief priests have delivered You to me. What have You done?" Jesus answered, "My kingdom is not of this world. If My kingdom were of this world, My servants would fight, so that I should not be delivered to the Jews; but now My kingdom is not from here."
Pilate therefore said to Him, "Are You a king then?"

Jesus answered, "You say rightly that I am a king. For this cause I was born, and for this cause I have come into the world, that I should bear witness to the truth. Everyone who is of the truth hears My voice." Pilate said to Him, "What is truth?"

—John 18:33–38a

$\mathcal{D}ay$ 26 - The Conclusion of the Fourth Trial of Jesus

～১৩～

Jesus presented Pilate with a choice—the same choice He offers us: compromise what you know to be truth and preserve your place in the kingdom of Tiberius, or walk in the light of truth and receive unseen rewards in God's kingdom. Apparently, the

bruises around Jesus' eyes didn't make the latter option especially attractive.

> *And when he had said this, he went out again to the*
> *Jews, and said to them, "I find no fault in Him at all."*
> —John 18:38b

Pilate probably wondered how these conundrums always
seemed to find him despite his best effort to remain neutral.
With Sejanus dead, he would not likely survive another contro-
versy. Yet there stood before him a man clearly not guilty of any
crime against Rome and a riotous crowd insisting He was a serious threat to Tiberius. They had appealed to Rome many times
and always seemed to gain the upper hand. And the last letter he
received from Tiberius made it clear he had better respect the
Jews' religious sensibilities or suffer the end of his career.

> *But they were the more fierce, saying, "He stirs up the*
> *people, teaching throughout all Judea, beginning from*
> *Galilee to this place."*
> —Luke 23:5

As Pilate sat reeling in yet another impossible political
quandary, a single word rose above the clamor to offer him
hope: *Galilee.* Jesus was from Galilee!

Not far away from the Praetorium, Herod Antipas, the
tetrarch of Galilee, had taken up residence for the Passover celebration. The Jewish aristocracy recognized him as a leader.
The jurisdiction was his. It was a perfect way to pawn the problem off on someone else.

$\mathcal{D}ay$ 27 - The Fifth Trial of Jesus

When Herod saw Jesus, he was greatly pleased, because for a long time he had been wanting to see him. From what he had heard about him, he hoped to see him perform some miracle. He plied him with many questions, but Jesus gave him no answer. The chief priests and the teachers of the law were standing there, vehemently accusing him. Then Herod and his soldiers ridiculed and mocked him. Dressing him in an elegant robe, they sent him back to Pilate. That day Herod and Pilate became friends—before this they had been enemies.

—Luke 23:8–12 NIV

Herod Antipas was the son of Herod the Great and had inherited many of his qualities, among them a great love of building an especially cruel disposition. Despite an impressive list of buildings and cities to his credit—including a capital city named for Tiberius—Antipas was a caricature of Roman debauchery.

Antipas cleverly balanced his Roman ties with the appearance of loyalty to his people. During several of the controversies with Pilate, he had advocated for the Jewish leaders and had successfully brought the wrath of Tiberius to bear. This made him an important potential ally for Pilate, who needed a powerful friend. Pilate knew that Herod *"had been wanting to see [Jesus]. From what he had heard about him, he hoped to see him perform some miracle"* (Luke 23:8 NIV). So, in a gesture not unlike a good-natured practical joke, he sent "the King of the Jews" to Herod for judgment.

If Antipas wanted a show, he was disappointed. Jesus recognized a basic fact of life: words are wasted on people who have no desire for truth. Earlier He referred to this as *"cast your pearls before swine"* (Matthew 7:6). Jesus' enemies hurled accusations while Herod cajoled Him for a display of miracles, but He remained silent. Eventually, Herod and his court grew tired of the game and sent Jesus back to Pilate. While he refused to take the problem off Pilate's hands, Herod acknowledged the procurator's joke by returning Jesus draped in a royal robe from his own collection.

As a result of the laugh the two men shared, Pilate gained the ally he so desperately needed. Nevertheless, Jesus remained his problem.

Day 28 - The Sixth—and Final—Trial of Jesus

Then Pilate, when he had called together the chief priests, the rulers, and the people, said to them, "You have brought this Man to me, as one who misleads the people. And indeed, having examined Him in your presence, I have found no fault in this Man concerning those things of which you accuse Him; no, neither did Herod, for I sent you back to him; and indeed nothing deserving of death has been done by Him. I will therefore chastise Him and release Him" (for it was necessary for him to release one to them at the feast).

And they all cried out at once, saying, "Away with this Man, and release to us Barabbas"—who had been thrown into prison for a certain rebellion made in the city, and for murder. Pilate, therefore, wishing to release Jesus, again called out to them. But they shouted, saying, "Crucify Him, crucify Him!" Then he said to them the third time, "Why, what evil has He done? I have found no reason for death in Him. I will therefore chastise Him and let Him go."

But they were insistent, demanding with loud voices that He be crucified. And the voices of these men and of the chief priests prevailed. So Pilate gave sentence that it should be as they requested. And he released to them the one they requested, who for rebellion and murder had been thrown into prison; but he delivered Jesus to their will.

—Luke 23:13–25

In a cell not far from the Praetorium judgment seat, a man waited for execution. One can only wonder how he came to be known as Barabbas. His name was nonsensical, meaning "son of a father." Perhaps it was an alias, a clever "John Doe" he had adopted to protect his family when he joined a band of thugs and eventually became their leader. By the time he was caught, he had become a notorious killer, the kind of criminal Romans delighted to execute using the most agonizing means possible. He was soon to be crucified.

This gave Pilate an idea. A custom of his predecessors had been to release one prisoner in honor of the Jewish festival. If he forced them to choose between an innocent man and one proven guilty of numerous crimes against Rome, certainly they wouldn't support a genuine enemy of the state. Choosing to release a renowned insurrectionist would put them on the opposite side of the issue from Caesar. But Pilate underestimated their hatred for Jesus. When he made the offer for them to choose between the two, they shouted, to his surprise, "Not this Man, but Barabbas!" (John 18:40).

Pilate's ploy not only failed to release him from the political web, but it entangled him further. Reluctant to pardon a notorious murderer, Pilate decided to scourge Jesus in order to spare Him the cross, hoping that "the halfway death" would satisfy the Jewish leaders' thirst for blood.

Day 29 - The Scourge of Jesus

So then Pilate took Jesus and scourged Him. And the soldiers twisted a crown of thorns and put it on His head, and they put on Him a purple robe. Then they said, "Hail, King of the Jews!" And they struck Him with their hands. Pilate then went out again, and said to them, "Behold, I am bringing Him out to you, that you may know that I find no fault in Him."

Then Jesus came out, wearing the crown of thorns and the purple robe. And Pilate said to them, "Behold the Man!" Therefore, when the chief priests and officers saw Him, they cried out, saying, "Crucify Him, crucify Him!"

Pilate said to them, "You take Him and crucify Him, for I find no fault in Him." The Jews answered him, "We have a law, and according to our law He ought to die, because He made Himself the Son of God."

Therefore, when Pilate heard that saying, he was the more afraid, and went again into the Praetorium, and said to Jesus, "Where are You from?" But Jesus gave him no answer. Then Pilate said to Him, "Are You not speak-

ing to me? Do You not know that I have power to crucify You, and power to release You?"

Jesus answered, "You could have no power at all against Me unless it had been given you from above. Therefore the one who delivered Me to you has the greater sin."

From then on Pilate sought to release Him, but the Jews cried out, saying, "If you let this Man go, you are not Caesar's friend. Whoever makes himself a king speaks against Caesar."

When Pilate therefore heard that saying, he brought Jesus out and sat down in the judgment seat in a place that is called The Pavement, but in Hebrew, Gabbatha. Now it was the Preparation Day of the Passover, and about the sixth hour. And he said to the Jews, "Behold your King!" But they cried out, "Away with Him, away with Him! Crucify Him!"

Pilate said to them, "Shall I crucify your King?"

The chief priests answered, "We have no king but Caesar!" Then he delivered Him to them to be crucified. Then they took Jesus and led Him away.

—John 19:1–16

Scourging involved the use of a *flagrum*, a whip with long, leather tails. The leather straps could be merely knotted or, if the *lictor*—a trained expert in the art of torture—wanted to inflict more damage, he could choose one with small, metal weights or even bits of sheep bone braided into the straps. "The iron balls would cause deep contusions, and the leather thongs and sheep bones would cut into the skin and subcutaneous tissues. Then as the flogging continued, the lacerations would tear into the underlying skeletal muscles and produce quivering ribbons of bleeding flesh."[5] The Romans were experts in the art of torture and knew exactly how to beat a man within an inch of his life. The procedure usually sent the victim into shock in less than five minutes and then took months to heal.

As the lictor chained Jesus' wrists to either side of a low wooden pillar, the entire cohort in the garrison filled the gallery to become a part of the humiliating spectacle. They jeered and hurled insults as the lictor chose his instrument, drew back, and snapped the weighted leather tails across Jesus' back. Jewish scourging limited the number of blows to thirty-nine and restricted the area to the back and shoulders, but Roman lictors were not given any rules. Back, legs, buttocks, chest, abdomen, face—no part of the body was off limits, and the beating could continue as long as everyone was entertained. And if the victim passed out, the lictor waited until he was conscious again before resuming the sadistic torture.

In the case of Jesus, the soldiers twisted together a crown of thorns and pressed it down on His head. They followed the humiliating coronation with more beating. They threw an officer's cape over Jesus' flayed shoulders as a royal robe, thrust a measure rod in His hands to be His scepter, and bowed before Him in mock reverence. "Hail, King of the Jews!"

Day 30 - The Journey to the Cross
～◌◌～

Now as they led Him away, they laid hold of a certain man, Simon a Cyrenian, who was coming from the country, and on him they laid the cross that he might bear it after Jesus. And a great multitude of the people followed Him, and women who also mourned and lamented Him. But Jesus, turning to them, said, "Daughters of Jerusalem, do not weep for Me, but weep for yourselves and for your children. For indeed the days are coming in which they will say, 'Blessed are the barren, wombs that never bore, and breasts which never nursed!' Then they will begin to say to the mountains, 'Fall on us!' and to the hills, 'Cover us!' For if they do these things in the green wood, what will be done in the dry?"

—Luke 23:26–31

After the *lictor* completed his cruel task, the *exactor mortis* and the *quaternio* stripped the prisoner naked and forced him to carry the implement of his own demise to the place of execution. They hung a sign, called a *titulus*, around his neck. The *titulus* was nothing more than a crude board inscribed with the prisoner's name and a list of his crimes. It would eventually be attached to the cross above his head to let everyone know why he hung there to die.

Having placed the burden of death on his back and the *titulus* around his neck, the *quaternio* formed a square around the victim and began a long, slow march through the main parts of the city—a death march called, in later years, the Via Dolorosa, the "way of suffering." The purpose of the march was, of course, to enhance the public spectacle which reinforced the warning to any other would-be criminals.

During the final trial, the *lictor* and his cohort had thrashed Jesus nearly to death. They sent Him back to the Praetorium bleeding, bruised, and trembling with shock. By the time Pilate handed Him over to the *exactor mortis,* Jesus would not have been able to carry His burden very far. He perhaps dragged it for some distance, but the soldiers became impatient and conscripted a man named Simon of Cyrene to carry it for Him.

Day 31 - The King on the Cross

When they reached a place the locals had nicknamed Golgotha, "Place of the Skull," they laid the *patibulum* on the ground and attached it to the top of the *stipes*. The victim was placed on top of the wood and attached to the cross, with his arms outstretched and feet flat against the face of the *stipes*. Usually, the victim was tied in place, which doesn't sound particularly brutal until you consider that he took much longer to die than when nailed.

To hasten the end, the *exactor mortis* could suspend the victim using nails instead of rope, which caused death within hours instead of days. Whereas the victim suffered for a shorter time, the intensity of his agony can barely be imagined. Physicians have determined through a combination of means that the victim would have been nailed to the cross through the hand at the base of the palm and at an angle so that the nail exited the wrist. This not only supported the weight of the person, but it also caused him the greatest amount of pain.

The nail, driven through the palm of the hand close to the wrist, severely damaged the median nerve of the arm and forearm. Within a couple of hours, the victim experienced an affliction known as *causalgia*.

A victim nailed to a cross, like someone tied in place, also had to keep his body in constant motion to relieve the pain in his arms, chest, and legs, which only agitated the damaged nerves in the nail wounds. Later, as fatigue set in, breathing would have been difficult, requiring more and more effort.

The soldiers took Jesus to Golgotha and initiated the gruesome ritual, which began with giving the victim a mild painkiller. This was no act of mercy. The process of nailing a person's limbs to a wooden beam is easier if he's drugged. Jesus refused the medicine, probably preferring to remain completely lucid during His ordeal.

Day 32 - The Crucifixion

Shortly after nine o'clock Friday morning, Jesus hung a few feet above the earth between two robbers—probably accomplices of Barabbas, who were surprised to see another man hanging on his cross. They had no doubt heard of Jesus and could guess what had happened by listening to the taunts of the religious leaders.

> *And those who passed by blasphemed Him, wagging their heads and saying, "Aha! You who destroy the temple and build it in three days, save Yourself, and come down from the cross!" Likewise the chief priests also, mocking among themselves with the scribes, said, "He saved others; Himself He cannot save. Let the Christ, the King of Israel, descend now from the cross, that we may see and believe."*
> *Even those who were crucified with Him reviled Him.*
> *—Mark 15:29–32*

The brigands on either side of Jesus joined the others taunting Him while the soldiers helped themselves to what few possessions the prisoners had. When they came to Jesus' clothing, they noticed that His tunic was unique in that it had been woven as one piece. Rather than ruin the garment, the men cast lots—rolled dice as it were—to determine who should keep it. Then, as the soldiers gambled and the religious leaders mocked, something changed within one of the robbers.

> *Then one of the criminals who were hanged blasphemed Him, saying, "If You are the Christ, save Yourself and us." But the other, answering, rebuked him, saying, "Do you not even fear God, seeing you are under the same condemnation? And we indeed justly, for we receive the due reward of our deeds; but this Man has done nothing wrong." Then he said to Jesus, "Lord, remember me when You come into Your kingdom."*
>
> *And Jesus said to him, "Assuredly, I say to you, today you will be with Me in Paradise."*
>
> —Luke 23:39–43

The religious leaders continued their taunts, quoting Scripture as they watched their Messiah suffer. *"He trusted in God; let Him deliver Him now if He will have Him; for He said, 'I am the Son of God'"* (Matthew 27:43).

At about noon, roughly three hours after the crucifixion began and when the sun should have been high overhead, an eerie darkness enveloped the entire region until three in the afternoon. As the darkness began to lift, Jesus drew a deep breath and shouted in Aramaic, His native tongue, *"My God, My God, why have You forsaken Me?"* (Matthew 27:46). Those who only spoke Greek or Latin struggled to make sense of His words, but the chief priests and scribes understood completely. Jesus was quoting a psalm written by the prophet-king, David, centuries before crucifixion had been invented.

The taunts continued as blood seeped from Jesus' wounds and ran down the cross to mingle with the soil. When He called for something to drink, someone put a sponge on the end of a branch of hyssop, dipped it in a jar of "sour wine," the drink "given with meals to soldiers and workers"[6] as an aid in reducing fever and giving refreshment. After drinking from the sponge, Jesus decided the work He came to do had been completed. He tilted His head back, pulled up one last time to draw a deep breath, and cried, *"Tetelestai!"*

With Jesus' last breath on the cross, He declared the debt of sin canceled, completely satisfied. Nothing else required. Not good deeds. Not generous donations. Not penance or confession or baptism or ... or ... or ... nothing. The penalty for sin is death, and we were all born hopelessly in debt. He paid our debt in full by giving His life so that we might live forever.

Day 33 - The Death of Hope

Now behold, there was a man named Joseph, a council member, a good and just man. He had not consented to their decision and deed. He was from Arimathea, a city of the Jews, who himself was also waiting for the kingdom of God. This man went to Pilate and asked for the body of Jesus. Then he took it down, wrapped it in linen, and laid it in a tomb that was hewn out of the rock, where no one had ever lain before. That day was the Preparation, and the Sabbath drew near.

And the women who had come with Him from Galilee followed after, and they observed the tomb and how His

*body was laid. Then they returned and prepared spices
and fragrant oils. And they rested on the Sabbath according to the commandment.*

—Luke 23:50–56

After the death of Jesus had been confirmed by the
centurion's spear and reported to Pilate, two important members of the Jewish ruling council, Joseph of Arimathea and
Nicodemus, requested His body. These formerly secret disciples, along with several women, would do the gruesome task
of preparing His corpse for burial. Once the soldiers lowered
the body of Jesus from the cross, His friends would have to
flex and massage His arms in order to relieve rigor mortis,
which kept the arms stuck in the V position after death. Then
they would wash His body and anoint it with oil before wrap-
ping it in a single linen cloth. A separate napkin tied under
His chin kept His mouth from gaping open after the muscles
began to loosen.

Next, they were to wrap His body from head to toe in long
strips of linen, which had been soaked in a mixture of spiced
resin. They would use seventy-five to one hundred pounds of
heavily scented spices to offset the smell of decomposition.
Then they would have laid Him on a shelf in a tomb excavated
from the side of a limestone hill or mountain. After a year had
passed and the body had completely decayed, they would have
gathered His bones and placed them in a family ossuary—a
bone box—along with those of His ancestors. Thus, He would
have been "gathered unto His fathers."

$\mathcal{D}ay\ 34$ - The Tomb Is Secured

The followers of Jesus did their best to complete their tasks before sundown in honor of the Sabbath, the Sadducees and Pharisees were hard at work petitioning Pilate once again.

> *"Sir, we remember, while He was still alive, how that deceiver said, 'After three days I will rise.' Therefore command that the tomb be made secure until the third day, lest His disciples come by night and steal Him away, and say to the people, 'He has risen from the dead.' So the last deception will be worse than the first."*
>
> —Matthew 27:63–64

Pilate didn't care what people believed, and he didn't see how a fake resurrection should be of any concern to Rome. So he gave the religious leaders an official seal to place on the grave and suggested they post their own guard, which likely consisted of Roman soldiers paid through the temple treasury and temple guards assigned to supervise the gravesite details. Having sealed the tomb and posted a company of guards by the entrance, the chief priests, scribes, and Pharisees went to their respective homes to keep the law of the Sabbath. On Sunday morning, they would continue to observe the Feast of Unleavened Bread and prepare for the sacrifices of the closing convocation. Then, having silenced Jesus . . . it was business as usual.

$\mathcal{D}ay$ *35* - He Is Risen

The morning after the Sabbath—Sunday morning—the guards stood watch over their dead prisoner when, suddenly, the ground shook and a brilliant light flooded the garden.

> *And behold, there was a great earthquake; for an angel of the Lord descended from heaven, and came and rolled back the stone from the door, and sat on it. His countenance was like lightning, and his clothing as white as snow. And the guards shook for fear of him, and became like dead men.*
>
> —Matthew 28:2–4

Sometime later, Mary Magdalene, another Mary, Salome, Joanna, and some other women converged on the tomb of Jesus. Luke's account reveals that their purpose was to complete the burial process with the spiced resin they had prepared (Luke 24:1) and that they even wondered how they would remove the giant stone. As Mary Magdalene and the women approached the tomb, they saw that the giant stone had been tossed aside and the guards were lying unconscious nearby. According to the Gospel by John, Mary Magdalene immediately ran to tell Peter and John what she thought had happened. *"They have taken away the Lord out of the tomb, and we do not know where they have laid Him"* (John 20:2).

While Mary Magdalene ran to tell Peter and John that someone had broken into the tomb, the other women moved in for a closer look.

*Then they went in and did not find the body of the Lord
Jesus. And it happened, as they were greatly perplexed
about this, that behold, two men stood by them in shin-
ing garments. Then, as they were afraid and bowed their
faces to the earth, and they said to them, "Why do you
seek the living among the dead?"*

—Luke 24:3–5

The grave was gaping open. The grave wrappings lay there,
still together and intact, but empty. The body was gone. The
original Greek describes the women "without a way," meaning
they were at a complete loss to explain the mystery. They stood
dumbstruck and staring for several moments, until they real-
ized that two angels appeared behind them. One sat on the stone
while the other stood nearby.

*"Why do you seek the living among the dead? He is not here,
but is risen! Remember how He spoke to you when He was
still in Galilee, saying, 'The Son of Man must be delivered into
the hands of sinful men, and be crucified, and the third day
rise again.'" And they remembered His words.*

—Luke 24:5b–8

*"[The women] went out quickly and fled from the tomb, for
they trembled and were amazed. And they said nothing to anyone, for they were afraid"* (Mark 16:8). But then they encoun-
tered someone who removed any doubt that might have
lingered in their minds.

*And as they went to tell His disciples, behold, Jesus met
them, saying, "Rejoice!" So they came and held Him by*

*the feet and worshiped Him. Then Jesus said to them, "Do
not be afraid. Go and tell My brethren to go to Galilee,
and there they will see Me."*

—Matthew 28:9–10

Day 36 - Continued

While Mary the mother of James, Salome, Joanna, and the other
women informed several of the disciples, Mary Magdalene located Peter and John. At first, they, too, dismissed her story as
hyperemotionalism, but curiosity eventually got the better of
them and they raced to the tomb.

*So they both ran together, and the other disciple outran
Peter and came to the tomb first. And he, stooping down
and looking in, saw the linen cloths lying there; yet he did
not go in. Then Simon Peter came, following him, and
went into the tomb; and he saw the linen cloths lying
there, and the handkerchief that had been around His
head, not lying with the linen cloths, but folded together
in a place by itself.*

—John 20:4–7

Peter ran straight into the tomb without stopping and "saw"
the linen wrappings differently. John used *theoreo,* from which
we derive the English word *theory.* Unlike John, Peter not only
observed the grave clothes, but he studied them for clues and
tried to comprehend what might have happened.

After Peter and John left the tomb to tell their respective households that Jesus had risen, Mary Magdalene had an extraordinary encounter of her own. The angels who had greeted the other women appeared to her as well (John 20:11–13). And as she left the garden, she saw the risen Jesus, who gave her the same instructions He gave the others: *Go find My brothers and tell them.*

Day 37 - The Upper Room

As Mary, Salome, Joanna, and the other women located the scattered followers of Jesus, and as word spread of His missing body, a multitude began to assemble in an upper room—perhaps the same room in which Jesus had celebrated the Passover. The followers discussed everything that had been reported by the women and bandied theories as to what might have happened. Peter and John arrived followed by Mary Magdalene and, before long, almost everyone who had been a close follower of Jesus found his or her way to the customary place of meeting, hoping to hear some more news.

Then, with the doors shut tight for fear of persecution and the followers engaged in animated conversation, a familiar voice rose from the middle of the room.

"Peace be with you." When He had said this, He showed them His hands and His side. Then the disciples were glad when they saw the Lord. So Jesus said to them again, "Peace to you! As the Father has sent Me, I also send you." And when He had said this, He breathed on

> them, and said to them, "Receive the Holy Spirit. If you
> forgive the sins of any, they are forgiven them; if you re-
> tain the sins of any, they are retained."

—John 20:19–23

When this occurred, Thomas, one of the Twelve, had not yet
returned from Galilee. When he arrived, everyone he met told
him the story of the empty tomb, and the bizarre way in which
the grave clothes were left, and the dazzling appearance of angels, and their personal encounter with the risen Jesus. Nevertheless, Thomas wouldn't believe the reports. *"Unless I see in
His hands the print of the nails, and put my finger into the print
of the nails, and put my hand into His side, I will not believe"*
(John 20:25).

With the doors shut tighter than before and the followers of
Jesus debating their next move, a familiar voice calmed the
room. *"Peace be with you."* Again Jesus stood in the middle of
the room, only this time He came to see one person in particular. Not to scold or to chastise or to shame . . . but to heal.
*"Reach your finger here, and look at My hands; and reach your
hand here, and put it into My side. Do not be unbelieving, but be-
lieving"* (John 20:27).

Thomas didn't move. He didn't even lift a finger. He didn't
argue or resist. He had been given everything he needed and
therefore responded as only a genuine follower of Jesus can respond. Thomas said, *"My Lord and my God!"*

Jesus replied, *"Thomas, because you have seen Me, you have
believed. Blessed are those who have not seen and yet have believed"* (John 20:28–29).

$\mathcal{D}ay$ 38 - On the Road to Emmaus

As the sun rose on Sunday morning and the Passover feast came to an end, two of Jesus' followers left for home, clearly disillusioned and resolving to leave their foolish dreams in Jerusalem forever. Even as rumors of resurrection circulated, the dejected pair began the seven-mile walk to the village of Emmaus.

> *And they talked together of all these things which had happened. So it was, while they conversed and reasoned, that Jesus Himself drew near and went with them. But their eyes were restrained, so that they did not know Him. And He said to them, "What kind of conversation is this that you have with one another as you walk and are sad?"*
>
> —Luke 24:14–17

Luke describes the disciples' conversation as bantering ideas back and forth with great emotion in a shared search for answers. When Jesus asked, *"What kind of conversation is this that you have with one another?"* (24:17), Luke uses the term *antiballo,* which literally means "to throw back and forth." The disillusioned followers desperately wanted to know why their expectations of the Messiah had come to such a tragic end, and so they were exploring a number of theories.

> *Then the one whose name was Cleopas answered and said to Him, "Are You the only stranger in Jerusalem, and have You not known the things which happened there in these days?"*
>
> —Luke 24:18

His question was laughable, given his audience. If anyone understood what had happened, it was Jesus! And if anyone was clueless, it was Cleopas! Nevertheless, Jesus encourages the disciples to talk, not to humiliate or chastise them, but for a very different purpose.

Day 39 - Belief Comes in Emmaus
✑✑✑

"What things?" So they said to Him, "The things concerning Jesus of Nazareth, who was a Prophet mighty in deed and word before God and all the people, and how the chief priests and our rulers delivered Him to be condemned to death, and crucified Him. But we were hoping that it was He who was going to redeem Israel."

—Luke 24:19–21

And with that statement, Cleopas revealed the source of his trouble. His noble expectations for a social, political, and economic Messiah had failed to materialize. His limited perspective would not allow him to embrace the Messiah's true agenda, of which economic prosperity and political liberation were only a tiny fraction. Cleopas's expectation yielded another tragic consequence.

[Cleopas continued,] "Indeed, besides all this, today is the third day since these things happened. Yes, and certain women of our company, who arrived at the tomb early, astonished us. When they did not find His body, they came saying that they had also seen a vision of angels who said He was alive. And certain of those who were

> *with us went to the tomb and found it just as the women
> had said; but Him they did not see."*
>
> —Luke 24:21–24

As they approached the town of Emmaus, the two disciples
found themselves so intrigued, they urged the stranger to stay
the night in keeping with ancient Near Eastern rules of hospi-
tality. Jesus accepted the offer, while maintaining His
anonymity. The disciples were not yet ready. One final truth-
obscuring layer remained on their eyes: they failed to ac-
knowledge the resurrection.

They had heard the reports; they had all the facts. They simply refused to believe with their whole hearts. And their lack of
belief affected everything. If these two disciples had believed
that Jesus was alive, they would have behaved differently in at
least two respects. First, they would have been walking *toward*
Jerusalem, where Jesus was last seen, not away. Second, they
would have accepted the trials, crucifixion, and burial of Jesus as
fulfillment of all He had promised, not as the end of their hopes.

As the afternoon sun drifted closer to the horizon, Jesus and
the two followers prepared the evening meal and, no doubt,
continued their discussion about the need for the Messiah to
die. Of course, the death of Jesus begged an obvious question.
"How, then, will the Messiah establish His kingdom and reign
over it if He's dead?"

> *Now it came to pass, as He sat at the table with them,
> that He took bread, blessed and broke it, and gave it to
> them. Then their eyes were opened and they knew Him;
> and He vanished from their sight.*
>
> —Luke 24:30–31

$\mathcal{D}ay$ *40* - Follow Me

On dozens of occasions over a forty-day period after His resurrection, Jesus appeared to hundreds of His disciples scattered across Judea and Galilee. He walked with them, shared meals, taught lessons, and enjoyed their company. He took this time to restore, reassure, and rejuvenate His citizens after they had suffered the traumatic experience of seeing their king tortured and killed. Many, if not most, had considered the Messiah's cause lost to evil and needed to be rallied for the work that lay ahead. He would prepare His followers in two mountaintop meetings. At the first meeting in Galilee, Jesus gave them the plan (Matthew 28:16–20); at the second in Judea, He gave them His power (Acts 1:3–11).

It was high on a mountain that God originally took Abraham, the father of the Hebrews, and said, *"To your descendants I will give this land"* (Genesis 12:7). The followers of Jesus must have thought He was about to renew God's covenant and tell them the plan by which they would claim the Promised Land for the new kingdom. And, in a way, He would. He presented His plan for kingdom-building clearly and simply. Many call this divine directive the "Great Commission."

Then the eleven disciples went away into Galilee, to the mountain which Jesus had appointed for them. When they saw Him, they worshiped Him; but some doubted.

And Jesus came and spoke to them, saying, "All authority has been given to Me in heaven and on earth. Go therefore and make disciples of all the nations, baptizing them in the name of the Father and of the Son and of the

Holy Spirit, teaching them to observe all things that I have commanded you; and lo, I am with you always, even to the end of the age." Amen.

—Matthew 28:16–20

The plan is to "make disciples of all nations."

Fortunately, God made all varieties of people with a wide variety of interests and abilities. He has called people of every race and color who have been hurt by life in every manner imaginable. Even the scars of past abuse and injury can be the means of bringing healing to another. What wonderful opportunities to make disciples!

Jesus commanded His followers to go and to be relentless in their making disciples, but He left the methods in our hands. Let me encourage you to be creative, then follow through with enthusiasm.

Notes

1. Gerhard Kittel, ed., *Theological Dictionary of the New Testament*, vol. 1, ed. And trans. Geoffrey W. Bromiley (Grand Rapids: Eerdmans, 1972), 185.
2. Ibid.
3. James Russell Lowell, "The Present Crisis" in *Poems by James Russell Lowell*, vol. 2 (Boston: Ticknor, Reed, and Fields, 1849), 57.
4. *International Standard Bible Encyclopedia*, Vol. 1 (Grand Rapids: Eerdmans, 1979), 128.
5. W.D. Edwards, MD, W.J. Gabel, MDiv, and F.E. Hosmer, MS "On the Physical Death of Jesus Christ," *The Journal of the American Medical Association* 255, no. 11 (21 March 1986): 1457.
6. Kittel, *Theological Dictionary of the New Testament*, 288.

STEPS TO PEACE WITH GOD

1. RECOGNIZE GOD'S PLAN—PEACE AND LIFE

The message in this book stresses that God loves you and wants you to experience His peace and life.

The BIBLE says ... For God loved the world so much that He gave His only Son, so that everyone who believes in Him may not die but have eternal life. John 3:16

2. REALIZE OUR PROBLEM—SEPARATION FROM GOD

People choose to disobey God and go their own way. This results in separation from God.

The BIBLE says ... Everyone has sinned and is far away from God's saving presence. Romans 3:23

3. RESPOND TO GOD'S REMEDY— THE CROSS OF CHRIST

God sent His Son to bridge the gap. Christ did this by paying the penalty of our sins when He died on the cross and rose from the grave.

The BIBLE says ... But God has shown us how much He loves us—it was while we were still sinners that Christ died for us! Romans 5:8

4. RECEIVE GOD'S SON—LORD AND SAVIOR

You cross the bridge into God's family when you ask Christ to come into your life.

The BIBLE says ... Some, however, did receive Him and believed in Him; so He gave them the right to become God's children. John 1:12

THE INVITATION IS TO:

REPENT (turn from your sins), ASK for God's forgiveness, and by faith RECEIVE Jesus Christ into your heart and life and follow Him in obedience as your Lord and Savior.

PRAYER OF COMMITMENT

"Dear Lord Jesus, I know that I am a sinner, and I ask for Your forgiveness. I believe You died for my sins and rose from the dead. I turn from my sins and invite You to come into my heart and life. I want to trust and follow You as my Lord and Savior. In Your Name, Amen."

If you are committing your life to Christ, please let us know!

Billy Graham Evangelistic Association
1 Billy Graham Parkway, Charlotte, NC 28201-0001
1-877-2GRAHAM (1-877-247-2426)
billygraham.org